Robert E. Lee

Wendy Conklin, M.A.

Table of Contents

Leading the South

Many historians believe Robert E. Lee was the finest leader in the Civil War. His sense of duty to his home made him a Southerner. He took risks and always tried to think of what his enemy would do next. His leadership gave the southern army courage and a purpose for fighting. A French leader, Napoleon Bonaparte, once said, "It is not men who make an army, but a man." No one fits this description better than Robert E. Lee.

Robert E. Lee

▼ Lee served as commander of the southern army.

Lee's Roots

Robert E. Lee was born in 1807 to a well-known Virginia family. His father had made a name for himself in the American Revolution. Lee's mother was very rich. Unfortunately, Lee's father spent most of the family's fortune.

Lee did well in school. He was especially good at mathematics. Also, it was obvious at an early age that he was a natural leader.

Lee enrolled in the military academy at West Point because it was free. While he was a student there, he made many friends. Some of these friends would fight against Lee in the Civil War.

Henry Lee

Light Horse Harry Lee

Lee's father was Henry Lee. He commanded cavalry (KAV-uhl-ree) during the American Revolution. He crept behind enemy lines with a "light" load of supplies. That's how he earned the nickname "Light Horse Harry" Lee.

▲ Young men went to West Point to train to be army officers.

Lee's First War

In 1846, the Mexican War started. This was a war with Mexico over the border of Texas. This was the first time Lee would have to show bravery in battle. He was an army **engineer** (en-je-NEAR). He built roads and bridges for the army. Lee did his job so well that he caught the eye of General Winfield Scott, the commander.

General Scott began having Lee **scout** for the army. On one scouting trip, Lee was almost caught by the enemy. He was near a spring when some Mexican soldiers came up for a drink. Lee had to hide underneath a fallen tree limb until they left.

General Winfield Scott led the United States troops across Mexico to capture the capital city and win the war.

Missing Home

In 1831, Lee married Mary Custis. She was the great granddaughter of Martha Washington. The Lees had seven children. When Lee was away during the Mexican War, he missed his family terribly.

Mary Custis Lee

▼ The Battle of Palo Alto was the first major battle in the Mexican War.

▲ Lee was very loyal to Virginia, his home state.

The Big Split

Robert E. Lee believed that slavery was wrong. He also did not want the South to **secede** (suh-SEED) from the Union. But, Lee loved his home state of Virginia.

In 1861, the country entered the Civil War. President Abraham Lincoln asked Lee if he would take command of the northern army. Lee stayed up all night trying to decide what to do. He paced the hallways of his home. It was a very difficult decision. In the end, Lee decided he had to defend his home state.

Lee **resigned** (ri-ZINED) from the United States Army. He had proudly served in the army for more than 30 years. He immediately began work with the **Confederate** (kuhn-FED-uhr-uht) Army.

▲ Lee's house in Virginia before the war

Leading West Point

After the Mexican War, Lee took charge of the military school at West Point. This was where men were trained to become officers in the army. Many of the top officers from both the North and the South attended this school.

▲ This sketch shows West Point around 1850.

Working for Jefferson Davis

Jefferson Davis was the president of the Confederate States of America, or the CSA. When the Southerners chose him to be their president, he picked men from West Point to lead the army. Davis chose Lee to be his war **advisor**. Lee did not spend time on the battlefield. Instead, he ordered troops to go from place to place.

The inauguration of Jefferson Davis as president of the CSA

Jefferson Davis

General Joseph Johnston commanded the Army of Northern Virginia. This was the South's main army. Johnston and Lee were friends. They had fought together during the Mexican War. When Johnston was injured, President Davis put Lee in command.

Which Army?

The Army of Northern Virginia was first called the Confederate Army of the Potomac. However, the northern army was called the Army of the Potomac. Lee renamed the southern army to avoid confusion.

▼ This was Lee's house in Richmond, Virginia, when he worked for Jefferson Davis.

General Joseph Johnston

The Seven Days' Battle

Lee knew that his most important job was to protect the southern capital of Richmond, Virginia. In May 1862, Lee sent his cavalry to spy on the northern army. Jeb Stuart led the southern cavalry. Stuart took 1,200 troops on a three-day scouting trip. They scouted General McClellan's northern army.

Lee used Stuart's information to help him defend Richmond. Lee attacked McClellan's army. The two sides fought five battles in seven days. These battles were called the Seven Days' Battle.

Even though McClellan won four of the five battles, he backed away from Lee's army. Lee proved his skill as a commander on the field in these battles. Lee made it clear that he would defend by attacking first.

▼ Jeb Stuart on horseback

▼ This map shows the region around the Confederate capital.

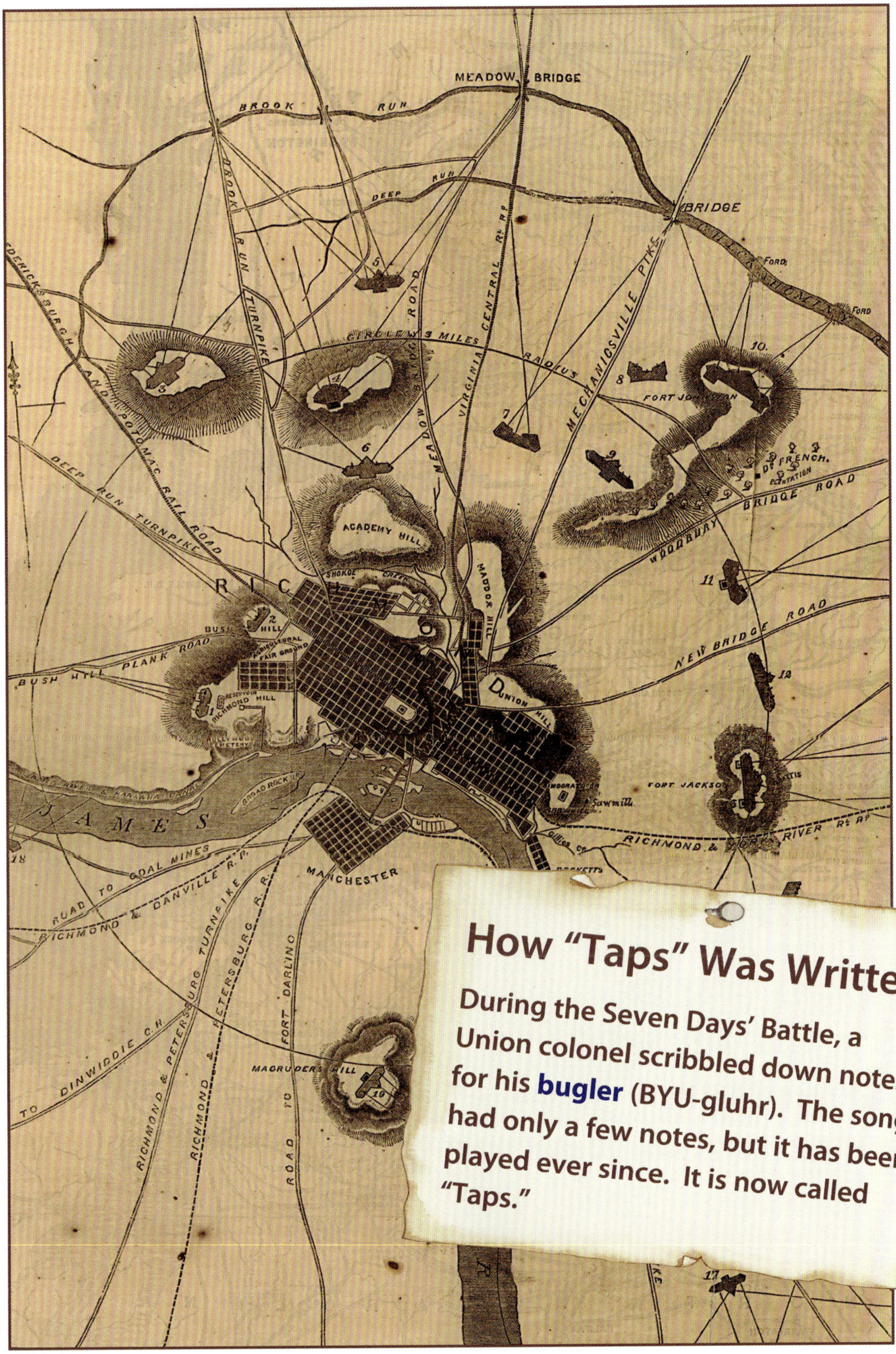

How “Taps” Was Written

During the Seven Days’ Battle, a Union colonel scribbled down notes for his **bugler** (BYU-gluhr). The song had only a few notes, but it has been played ever since. It is now called “Taps.”

The Battle of Second Manassas

Lee relied heavily on a few generals. He called Thomas "Stonewall" Jackson his "right arm." This meant that Lee trusted Jackson. James Longstreet was Lee's "old war horse." Lee could trust Longstreet to always be there for the army.

Lee used both Longstreet and Jackson at the Battle of Second Manassas (muh-NAS-uhs). This battle took place in August 1862. Lee sent Jackson's men in front of the Union Army. Then he ordered Longstreet to secretly attack from the side. At the same time, Jeb Stuart raided the northern army from behind.

Jackson's men took quite a beating. But, Longstreet attacked just in time. Shocked, the northern army fled. Time and time again, Lee had these leaders carry out his aggressive plans.

General James Longstreet

General Thomas Jackson

Jackson's Foot Cavalry

General Jackson's men marched fast and hard from place to place. Other troops started calling them the "foot cavalry." Jackson was a well-respected general.

▼ Manassas, Virginia, was the sight of two major battles.

Battling for Antietam

General Lee's next big battle took place in Maryland. This was the first battle on northern soil. The Union General George McClellan had three times more men than Lee. However, McClellan thought that Lee had more troops. Lee was a good judge of character and knew McClellan would hesitate. Lee was right.

The Battle of Antietam took place on September 17, 1862. This was the bloodiest day in American history. Both sides

▼ Terrible fighting at the Battle of Antietam

lost thousands of soldiers. Almost 21,000 men were killed or wounded that day.

Even after such terrible fighting, Lee refused to **retreat**. His army waited during the next day for an attack. McClellan's army was stronger. The Union soldiers could have attacked the weakened Southerners. McClellan did not attack. So, Lee's army was able to return to the South.

General George McClellan

Lee's Orders

A Union soldier discovered papers wrapped around some cigars. On the papers were the secrets of Lee's plans as he moved into Maryland. The papers were given to General McClellan, but he still hesitated in moving his troops to defeat Lee's army. President Abraham Lincoln was upset by McClellan's careful strategies.

Tragic Chancellorsville

In the spring of 1863, a battle took place in Chancellorsville, Virginia. The Union Army outnumbered Lee's army again. The new northern general was Joseph Hooker. He knew he had more men and a stronger army than Lee. The Union Army expected to overpower the Southerners. General Hooker and his men attacked. When Lee did not retreat, General Hooker panicked. He ordered his army to stop the attack and move back.

Another Smart Move

There was a big battle in the cold winter months late in 1862. This took place at Fredericksburg, Virginia. The Northerners **occupied** the town. Lee's army was dug in on the high ground just outside of town. The Union Army attacked the well-positioned Southerners. The Southerners fired down on the Union soldiers. The Northerners had no chance and thousands were killed.

▲ The Battle of Chancellorsville tested the northern leaders again.

Other northern leaders were angry. They thought they had an advantage. Hooker was being too careful and it would cost them.

Generals Jackson and Lee came up with a risky plan. They decided to have Jackson take his men away from Lee. Jackson would march around to the right side of the northern army. The Southerners could then attack the northern army on two sides. This would surprise the enemy. The plan worked. The northern army lost many soldiers in the attack.

The southern army paid a terrible price, too. A southern soldier shot Jackson by mistake. Jackson died a few days later. The Confederates lost one of their best leaders.

▲ **Lee and Jackson making plans on the battlefield at Chancellorsville**

The Battle of Gettysburg

Lee took a hard look at his men. They were tired and hungry. He created a plan to invade the North with his army. Lee wanted total victory, not just one more win.

At times, the cavalry acted like spies. They rode to where the other army was and scouted. Lee used Jeb Stuart's cavalry as his eyes and ears. At the end of June 1863, Stuart had not checked in with Lee for awhile. So, Lee did not know where the northern army was located. Union General George Meade and the Union Army were also moving North. A great battle was about to occur.

The two great armies met at Gettysburg, Pennsylvania. For three days, they fought in a huge battle. The Union Army held its position against the Confederates.

▼ **The final charge at the Battle of Gettysburg**

The Battle of Gettysburg was very important. This battle was considered the North's first major victory. From this point on, the northern army started winning more battles.

▼ **This map shows the battle lines of the two armies at Gettysburg.**

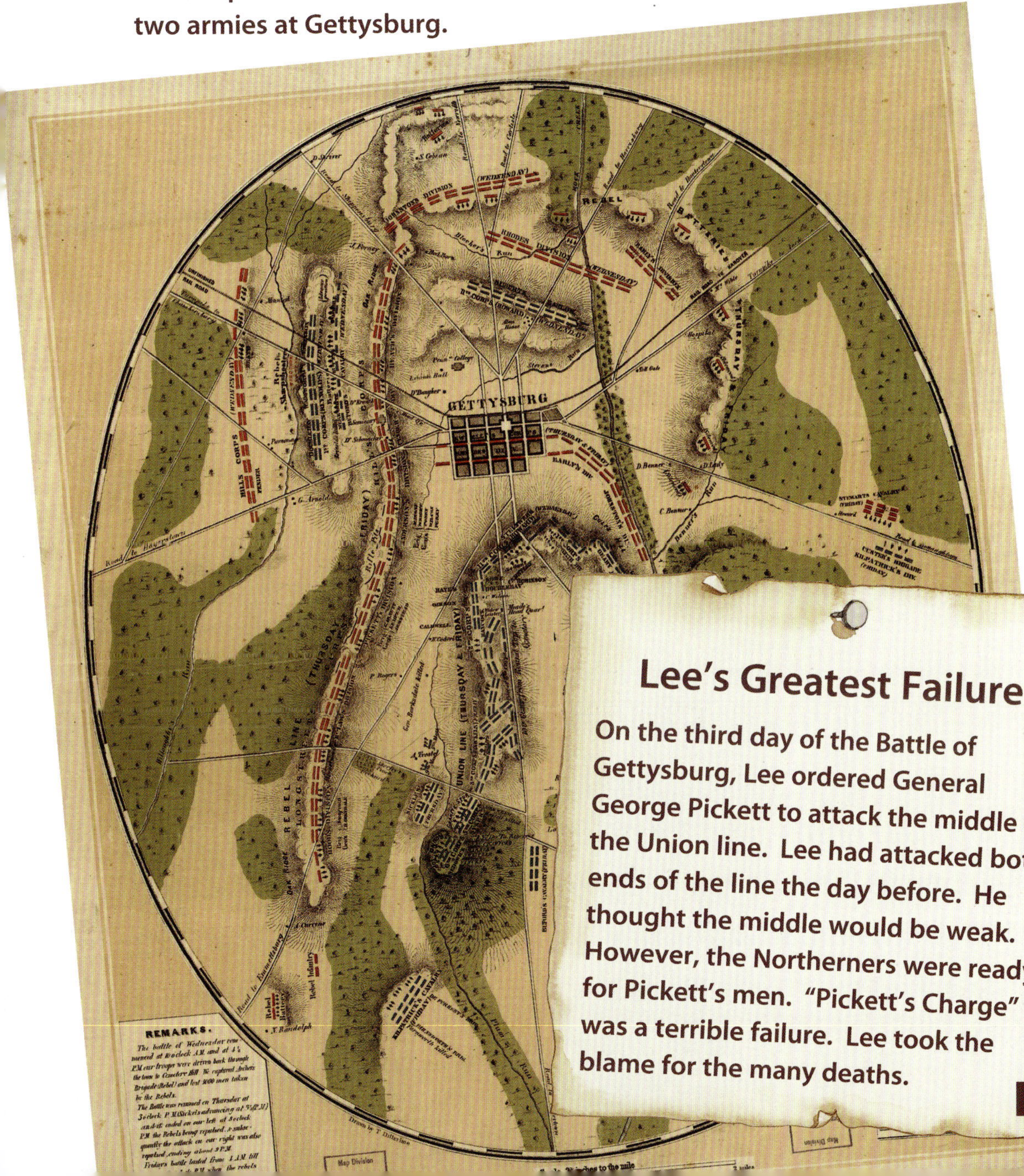

Lee's Greatest Failure

On the third day of the Battle of Gettysburg, Lee ordered General George Pickett to attack the middle of the Union line. Lee had attacked both ends of the line the day before. He thought the middle would be weak. However, the Northerners were ready for Pickett's men. "Pickett's Charge" was a terrible failure. Lee took the blame for the many deaths.

Losing Lee's Home

Lee's home was just across the river from Washington, D.C. When Lee left to fight for the Confederacy, he knew he might lose his land. In 1864, the United States government took control of the property because Mrs. Lee did not pay her taxes in person. The land was turned into a national cemetery so that the Lee family would never want to return to the property.

Lee in 1869 shortly before his death

Appomattox Court House

With few men and low supplies, Lee knew the end had come. By April 1865, the North had won at Petersburg and Richmond, Virginia. Lee hated to see his men suffer. His people had lost faith in their cause, and Lee knew that, too.

Lee said, "There is nothing left me but to go and see General Grant, and I would rather die a thousand deaths." He contacted the northern commanding general, Ulysses S. Grant. The two commanders met at a home in Appomattox (ap-uh-MAT-uhks) Court House, Virginia. Lee **surrendered** (suh-REN-duhrd) his army and ended the war.

At the time, even northern soldiers praised General Lee. When he walked by, they took off their hats and **saluted** him. When Lee died in 1870 of a **stroke,** all of America mourned his death. Robert E. Lee was a smart, noble man. He believed in the southern cause and defended his home as the leader of the Confederate Army.

▼ These men and women gathered at Lee's house after his funeral.

Glossary

advisor—someone who gives advice to another or keeps them informed

bugler—musician who used a musical instrument to play tunes for the military, each tune had a different meaning to the soldiers

cavalry—soldiers who ride horses in battle and are often scouts

Confederate—a person who supported the South in the Civil War

engineer—someone trained to build structures for the military

occupied—took over

resigned—gave up a job

retreat—to move away from the enemy in battle

saluted—raised a hand to show respect

scout—move ahead of the troops to map the land and discover where the enemy is located

secede—to break away from; states that left the Union

stroke—sickness that is caused when blood flowing to the brain is interrupted

surrendered—gave up and lost a battle or the war